THE WITCH WHO WENT FOR A WALK

Modern Curriculum Press
BEGINNING
TO
READ
Series

THE WITCH WHO WENT FOR A WALK

Margaret Hillert

Illustrated by Krystyna Stasiak

 MODERN CURRICULUM PRESS

Library of Congress Cataloging in Publication Data

Hillert, Margaret.
　The witch who went for a walk.

　(MCP beginning-to-read books)
　Summary: While taking a walk on Halloween night, a witch and her cat are frightened by three children in costumes.
　[1. Witches — Fiction.　2. Halloween — Fiction]　I. Stasiak, Krystyna.　II. Title.
PZ7.H558Wi　　[E]　　80-21433

ISBN 0-8136-5605-2 (paperback)
ISBN 0-8136-5105-0 (hardbound)

20　19　18　17　　　　　　　　　　06　05　04　03　02　01　00

Here I am.
Up, up, up.
Way up here.
See how I ride.

5

And see my cat.
He rides, too.
He is a good cat.
He helps me see.

6

7

8

We like it up here.
It is fun to ride up here.
We can look down.
Down, down, down.

It is fun up here.
But I want to go for a walk.
I guess I will go down
and have a look.

Here we are, cat.
Do you want to eat?
I will make you something
good to eat.

Now we will go for
a little walk.
Come on.
Come this way to see what we
can see.

14

Oh, oh.
What have we here?
Do you see what I see?
This is funny.

15

And look here.
Guess what we
will find in here.
Go in. Go in.

16

Look up, up, up.
See what is up there.
Something little.
Do you see that?

Now come out.
Walk, walk, walk.
I see something here, too.

I see friends.
One, two, three friends.
Oh, this is good.
I like to see friends.

But what is this?
Is it a friend?
No, no.
It is something funny.

20

It can not run.
It can not jump.
It sits and sits and sits.

I see something.
It looks like a cat.
It looks something like you.
What is it?

22

What are you?
I guess you are a cat.
But you are yellow!
My cat is not yellow.
You look funny.

I like this walk.
We look and look.
We have fun.

24

Now here is something.
Up here. Up here.
Who? Who?
Who are you?

O-o-o-o-h!
Look. Look.
Oh, my. Oh, my.
What is this?

E-e-e-e-e-e!
What is this?
I do not like this.
I do not like the way
you look.

29

No, no.
I do not like this.
Come away, cat. Come away.
We will have to go now.

Here we go.
Up, up, and away.
I guess a walk is not too
good for us.
This is the way to go.

31

Margaret Hillert, author of several books in the MCP Beginning-To-Read Series, is a writer, poet, and teacher.

The Witch Who Went for a Walk uses the 67 words listed below.

a	go	make	that
am	good	me	the
and	guess	my	there
are			this
away	have	no	three
	he	not	to
but	helps	now	too
	here		two
can	how	oh	
cat		on	up
come	jump	one	us
		out	
do	I		walk
down	in	ride(s)	want
	is	run	way
eat	it		we
		see	what
find	like	sits	who
for	little	something	will
friend(s)	look(s)		
fun			yellow
funny			you